A constellation of abnormalities

A constellation of abnormalities

Paul Cliff

PUNCHER & WATTMANN

First published in 2017
Published by Puncher and Wattmann
PO Box 441
Glebe NSW 2037

http://www.puncherandwattmann.com

puncherandwattmann@bigpond.com

National Library of Australia
Cataloguing-in-Publication entry:

Cliff, Paul

A constellation of abnormalities

ISBN   9781922186959

I. Title.

A821.3

Cover design by David Musgrave

cover art adapted by author from an old anatomical illustration

Contents

Snake-man

John Cann at La Perouse

Snakes either don't want to, or can't *learn*,
to love you. They go to ground, or strike, as they're wont —
whatever the snake-fit thing to do.
So who'd want to play with them?
Well, this fellow evidently:
shaking them out of their separate tied hessian sample-bags.
Each spilled tumbling onto the ground,
dropped like soiled washing at his thick boots ...
One breaks, and hightails it straight for the crowd
to create some frisson. (*It works.*)
But the Snake-man just calmly reaches out
and turns it neatly back on his long, metal stick:
looped like dangerous molasses on a spoon.
Then gives it time out, in a stout-lidded Tupperware box.

Using this stick like an inverse lightning-rod
that steers the strike away from him,
he continues to stir the snake-pot:
toppling more louts out
to strut their fine-snaky stuff by ones and twos;
untangling them like scaly syntax;
nudging them this way and that.
Correcting another errant one,
just when you think he's forgot.

It's like trying to herd lethal cats,
doing his slow-stepped skate around them —
keeping a sly, sideways eye peeled,
and cool count of what's out-and-about.
Being careful not to tread on their backs,

as he relates to us their particular temperaments —
habitats and range; their neurotoxic effect
on human nervous system and brain.
Working them over like holiday snaps,
to entertain us. This diligent showman-conjuror,
with the sun's sweat coiled tight at the small of his back.

Thanking us finally at the end,
and with pale, scarred fingers and hands,
passing around his sweat-stained hat.
Which he's removed like a gentleman-caller's,
in respectful token to these, his tempestuous loves.
The snakes.
Who don't, or won't — or simply *can't*,
in naked fact — love us.

Dogs

Dogs are always somewhere out there
in the neighbourhood. With their intractable yapping, sniffing —
scratching, crapping.
Running their ceaseless, private doggy-errands;
doing their doggy derring-dos.
You are essentially with them, or not:
> *Doggy*-People and *Non-Doggy*-People
> are one way of dividing this world.

Though personally wishing doggies no ill,
I could not be considered simpatico.
Not seeing any compelling (actual, *ipso facto*)
need for the existence of doggies —
being okay if they should all be banished from this earth,
or discreetly morphed into more of some animal-else.
> (As I sit here quietly thinking to myself: Christ,
> whose fucking dog is that barking in the street *now*,
> and why aren't its owners shutting it up!?)

One odd thing, mind, is that dog-folk can find
it hard to believe that you don't like dogs
> (especially theirs),
and inclined to try pushing them onto you.
With a touch of the self-righteous almost,
like the Jehovahs banging at your front door.
They make the mistake of assuming the doggy-loving position
as the natural human default:
that Non-Doggy folk are somehow emotionally stunted —
insecure, unevolved, or not at-peace with themselves.
> (People can be like that about having *children*, too.)
But that's a miscall — when half of the perfectly
healthy, normal workaday-folk of this earth

comprehensively just *don't* give a stuff for doggies.
(And a fringe-minority would as soon see the things
all put up and shot against a wall.)

Still, Doggy- and Non-Doggy folk need to work something out;
learn to tolerate each other's point of view.
To arrive at some kind of Doggy-Détente.
It's just a part of the inherent, ongoing complexity of our life on this earth,
and of building a better world.

Now — to the matter of *Cats*!

Himalayan rock salt

They are bringing the rock salt down:
all the way from the caves of the High Himalaya to me.
In fist-sized blocks — borne in sacks on the porters' backs,
with the porters cussing, stumbling
and cutting their poor, naked feet on the slippery scree.

They are bringing the rock salt down:
each man bowed with his one sack each;
watermarked with the sweat of his personal struggle with it —
as he passes under the cloud-shredding peaks,
edges past the sheer, thousand-metre drops.
(And under the eye of the snow leopard, perhaps,
if he's not imagining it: Up there, in that shadowy cleft?)
Then coming on to an especially dangerous stretch,
and really needing to concentrate,
where the bleached bones of the extinct aurochs are exposed.
And the ammonite fossil inscriptions in limestone
which are much more ancient still (from the time of that great,
primordial sea which gave its salt up) ...
Then they're gaining the tree line, to wend their way on
through the rhododendron forest, relieved to be out of the cutting
wind — then staggering on into the first ragged settlement,
where the villagers watch from their crooked doorways,
as they shuffle in single-file up the narrow street.

And so the porters persevere:
till at last their caravan's arrived here, in my front yard.
And they swing their heavy sacks down in the drive,
collapse to the lawn and drop onto their backs.
Then finally relax: sit idly bantering and chiacking each other
as they pass their flasks of *chhaang*
and light up their *beedi* cigarettes.

Some dabbing mercurochrome onto the soles of their feet
and binding them in cloth ...

As the neighbours' dogs bark at all this great unseemly commotion.
And passing cars slow, intrigued by this sight
in a suburban street. Honking their horns
in pure-naked delight and astonishment:
to acknowledge the porters' accomplishment,
courage, determination and strength —
in bringing the rock salt down.

> (And to exhort them maybe, now that they're here,
> to realise their fuller potential.
> Get an education, study a trade
> and build some sort of career) ...

As — with the evening coming on now —
the porters tear down the neighbour's paling fence
to contrive their night-fire
and make their *tsampa* and buttered tea ...
Then finally, under a starlight vastly less brilliant
than the one they are used to back home,
curl up on their sides in their blankets. And sleep.

As I watch through my kitchen window,
with the grinded salt cupped in my palm.
Tasting its pure, salt-sweet deliciousness on my tongue ...
every step of the arduous way it has come:
thoroughbred, unprocessed, with no bleached, supermarket taint.
Bearing the pedigree, pink bloodline of that ancient sea
which the mountains hijacked millennia ago.
The true, precious taste of this earth.

And the porters have brought the rock salt down —
all the way from the High Himalaya, to my table and me.

The Chinese House (Balibo)

'A young Chinese girl [who] had gone mad was in an animal corral at the back of the house, having been left behind when the civilian population fled'
— *Jill Jolliffe*, Balibo

The journalists died in the 'Chinese House'.
Which is not the house on the edge
of the small, grassy square on the Batugadé Road,
and maintained as a community-hall now.
(And on whose outside wall, as the old newsfilm shows,
Greg Shackleton daubed the flag,
underscored with the capital word: 'AUSTRALIA') —

but the house on the *Maliana* Road,
just below the old Portuguese fort on the hill —
the house where, by common report,
the Chinese man had kept his disturbed daughter
penned in an animal stall in the backyard.
With its windows and roof long-gone now.
And its broken, moss-stained walls —
outside of which the five had raised their hands
to call clearly, aloud:
          'Journalists! … Australians!'
before each being shot, bayoneted or knifed.
With their bodies then dragged
(and tossed, along with their film canisters)
into a pile of fuel-laced mattresses, and burned.

Three or four of the five slain together this way,
it's surmised (witness accounts are confused):
either in the street in front of the Chinese House,
or else its front room.
With the tall, bearded newsman murdered separately,
either in the house's bathroom —

or while attempting escape
through the rear of the Chinese House:

       scrambling past the spot where, by common report,
       the Chinese man abandoned his daughter,
       corralled in an animal stall in the backyard.

Song: *Plus ça change*

Plus ça change.
The more the world spins round on itself
in its peerless giddy-white-blue,
the more things stay the same —

with History like the dark face of the moon.
Hidden, chill, and fixed in a backward-staring rictus,
as the same dark deeds are repeated on ceaseless loop
in the same backroom.

As in Abu Ghraib now
the liberators do
what the despot once did:

And a slip of a West-Virginia farm-girl
in Army Reserve fatigues and oversize boots
reins a naked man down on a leash,
to kneel in his own excrement ...
And another man, with electrodes fixed to his fingertips,
is contrived to adopt a crucifix attitude
while balancing on a box
and wearing a hood.

As in Abu Ghraib now,
the liberators most assiduously do
precisely what the despot once did:

And the girl looks down on the naked man
sprawled on the prison floor in his collar and leash ...
And a large Alsatian full of Victory's teeth,
and straining on another leash,
goes: Woof! *Woof! WOOF!*

Always a dog barking somewhere

The dogs are barking — Again.
With perplexing urgency,
diligence, application and purpose.
As if presuming on us to join in with them;
or to at least come out and investigate,
show the vaguest human sympathy in their cause or affairs.

Barking, far into the night.
Without adding anything new at all to the world
(we've heard it all so often before).
Nor comprehending that their barking is actually something
we'd far vastly prefer to be without —
that it's all just so much unwanted (unwarranted) noise, to us.
Which inclines us to shut up our windows and doors,
shout a curse, or lob something unpleasant at them
to induce them to stop.

Yet still — in all their impossible, implausible,
incurable, romantic ignorance — they persist.
Bark unrepentantly on, in their grand incontinence ...
their sound echoing across land, sea and sky,
all the world's suburbs, fields, wastelands —
breeds, religions and tongues.

Till there simply seems to be no cure — either for it, them or us.

So these dogs bark remorselessly on.
Always a dog barking somewhere.

Three ekphrastic pieces

1 *Baigneuse*: Marthe bathes (again)

'Over the course of his lifetime Pierre Bonnard painted manifold versions of his wife bathing, always evoking her as a young woman even when they'd both grown old'

All these Marthes shown at her bath:
lolled soaking, stepping in or out,
poised stooped or upright.
In artful deployment of her towel,
or making some gentle inquisition of herself:
hands fumbling at the flesh-bouquet of her chest
or lifted tending her hair.
Her slender, deer-like shoulders, buttocks and flanks
sent ceaselessly into the great wash of this world:
flesh filtering the light like stained glass ...

So that Marthe might ask:

> Husband, our whole time together
> I've spent boiling water and fetching clean towels,
> as for births. How many times is a woman obliged
> to undress and step naked into her bath?
> Or a man to tease himself
> touching her body's flesh up with paint and brush,
> struggling to see it anew?
> Can so much body-washing be justified in this world?
> Any woman's flesh warrant such exacting watch?
>
> *Baigneuse* not being a profession
> I ever remotely imagined for myself as a girl:
> please tell me what this epic of incorrigible bathing
> has been about. When will the business stop?

And — with your eyes, never good,
and grown progressively worse,
to presently almost give out,
so I watch my body obliterate
into bright-broken lozenges of mosaic-like paint —
can you promise me that if I run the taps
to undress yet again for you now:
this will be the time where together, you and I,
finally get it right?

2 The human stain

'I keep laying it all over the floor until such time as it tells me what it wants to become' — Rosalie Gascoigne

Just give me the vital Things themselves:
as hunted-&-gathered, each taken up
humble and wonderful as it comes.
Uncensored, raw. Unadorned.
No marks placed upon them of mine,
just those of their pure, hard-lived, glorious selves:
       gnarled, dull, shiny, straight or warped,
       battered, scratched, scarred —
       marked with the haphazard break,
       ingrained with the human stain.
Incarnate with themselves:
       the enamel coffee pot with Dalmatian-spots of brown rust;
       old Schweppes crates sun-faded to lovely Renaissance tones;
       eloquent lengths of kinked fencing wire,
       swan feathers scabbed from the side of Lake George …
And assorted shelves, boxes and buckets full
of such bountiful junk-stuff more. Natural and man-made.

Yes — all that is scorned, trashed, forsaken, waylaid,
is for me pure, artful gain.
This jettisoned wonderland, magically tumbled to me:
maybe given just a short trim or nudge
to help kick matters along;
the slightest touch of a supervisory hand.
Just let me have those — some shed-space,
the instinct, patience and grace —
to allow them to coalesce: cohere,
          gravitate
               and fall into each other
to each speak their own genius-selves ...

As stacked, threaded, bound, sewn or hung —
glued, screwed, nailed, staplegunned —
or however appropriately fixed, devised or arranged,
and held up for the human regard.

3 McCubbin's *The Pioneer* (1904)

National Gallery of Victoria

McCubbin, in his big, ambitious, historical-narrative work
The Pioneer, invokes the in-vogue creed of nation-building:
with the colour green (forest/tent/dress/shirt) locking this in,
waltzing across the three big panels —

in the first and left-most of which the young wife is seen,
sitting slumped (dreamy? despondent?)
before a slackly pitched tent; with her husband crouched
setting kindling, behind.

In the second-and-middle panel, the bush is part-cleared:
the husband rests weary on a log with his axe,

while the wife stands before him shouldering a babe-in-arms,
and a slab-hut smokes in tender contentment to the rear.

Then climactically, in the final-and-third of the painting's panels
(with a taint of the comic, even —
in its sudden, dramatic, faintly hammy reverse),
the sky leeches blue through the green-dun frame of the eucalypts
to reveal a distant city-view
which brandishes real estate signs almost ...

as an innominate youth (the grown child or someone entirely else?)
is parting ferns, to disclose a simple bush grave.
Resting place of the pioneer-husband,
of his wife, their child — or who? ...
left behind at the previous century's turn,
as he kneels in the glittering scar of cleared ground,
pledged to the bright-shiny new.

Madame Butterfly braves the rain

Handa Opera, Sydney Harbour foreshore
for Jill

Rain can't faze a good Japanese soprano.
She'll sing up a storm as it streams down over
her white-painted forehead and into her almond eyes.
Back brazenly bared to reveal her butterfly-tattoo bodysuit.
Belting it out, before breaking off to flitter about-stage
in her treacherous *geta* sandals;
tripping her way up the steel ladder
and down the slippery stairs —
as Puccini peerlessly orchestrates
her exaltation and despair ...

And the harbour night teems with rain,
as behind her the *Celebrity Solstice*,
looking like one of the quayside tower-blocks
toppled, stunned, onto its side,
fiercely threshes to turn its high, bright-lit rump.
A few passengers poking their heads
from their cabin's balcony doors for a look,
before ducking them back into the glowing insides.
As Cio-Cio-San sings bravely on. Waterproof, it seems.
And we sit on the scaffolding's streaming bleachers,
cowed in our Opera-House ponchos,
numbly clutching our plastic flutes of champagne.
Barracking for her: the fearless soprano, Hiromi Omura.
Prevailing there at the harbour's edge in her sodden kimono.
A-singin' and a-singin' in the rain ...

'If the Hat Fits': Marianne Moore on the cover of the Faber *Collected*

The poet sits in sassy, high poise
        (or a kind of 'wry dudgeon'),
gazing off from under her outsized hat:
a high-crowned, straw-weave juggernaut,
stiff, lacquered and black,
brim broad as a Packard's running-board.
And fit cap for her wit and learning.

Mouth set with a sour, Mona-Lisa smile.
Tolerance tangoing with petulance
in the widdershins folds of her jowls.
As if she's sucking a hornet
crystallised in a sugar-cube, perhaps.
And that fierce eagle-eye soars
over the awry, unpredictable smile
of the budgie that swallowed the cat —
one thought scrambling quickly
up over another's back:
to signify that this lady will suffer fools *not*!
Is set to roll her sleeves right up
to give somebody or something
a damned healthy shake — slap, clout
or tongue-lash, as appropriate.
(Or equally, given due cause,
a kindly endorsement as much.)

Yes, the photograph on the *Collected*'s cover
somehow expresses all that;
with something intangibly Moore on top.
So you're struck with the thought that:

'Well yes, of course,
that's *exactly* how this lady would have to look.
I should have guessed that!'
The face fits the trope, the wry, sly-
            dropping rhyme,
                    the deft stab, twist-and-turn-
            over of the line —
and everything else.
This cover ably judges its book
to put the lady square at the scene of her crime,
in perfect poetic identikit ...

All set off (defined by),
and drawn in under the Saturn-sized pull of:
that preposterously wide-brimmed hat.

The eucalypt pod

After reading Hugh Kenner's 'The Pound Era'

Kenner relates how Pound, arrested on charges of treason in Rapallo, in May 1945, was marched downhill from his house into town, escorted by two tommy-gun bearing guards. And on the *salita*'s steep, sharp left-turn (just below Sant' Ambrogio) was allowed to rest in the shade of a large, Australian flowering gum. The tree thriving there, a favourite town rendezvous spot. Sustained by Mediterranean skies, soil and light, 19,000 kilometres from its native home.

And he'd gathered a seed pod up from the blossom-drenched ground, and pocketed it in his coat. Alongside his copy of Legge's *Confucius* and dictionary of Chinese ideograms. Then he and his guard had relinquished the tree's spawn-ground, with its freely dropped, scarlet-petalled pods scattered fiercely all around — to meander their way on. The three nattering between themselves: with a guard on each side, or even (who knows) both ambling along in front ...

And Kenner tells how, through the subsequent months of his Pisa trial, Pound protected this pod from the marauding cats slipping in through the bars of his holding-cage in the prison grounds. But doesn't tell whether or not, following his conviction and extradition to the States, Pound kept hold of it to sustain himself in the ward at St Elizabeths.

This hard, bullet-shaped pod — with its metal-coloured jacket and delicate scarlet flower. Frail remembrance, keepsake, of the pre-war years and Rapallo ... Ammunition for holding out against the protracted assaults on his reputation; the decades of his ongoing ruin.

Harry Flashman at the Hotel Santo

Luganville, Espiritu Santo island, Vanuatu

Somehow I always knew I'd fetch up somewhere rum like this. Some
ragged-tailed paradise, crawling with Adventist-&-Presbyterian
religious, at the scrag-end of the Imperial World. Renting some
poxy hotel backroom, to muddle it at Happy Hour with the yachties
and Harvey World package-tourists — oddball environmentalists;
failed, dream-scheming entrepreneurs. Braying packs of loud-
mouthed Australians on diving tours — and all the other parboil-
brained creatures of this earth... With the kill-joy pastors warning
their pretty parishioners off the aged Lothario of me, as the frisky
fillies and lovely young mares trip their way to Sunday church:
white-covered Gospels clasped in silky-black hands; rounded
haunches riding high, full-and-sassy under their Mother Hubbard
skirts.

Sweet Christ, to be exiled here! Botting cigarettes and cheap
whiskies in exchange for my crooked tales of contrived self-glory
so riddled with falsehood and exaggeration from all the years of
their telling that I can hardly untangle the truth for myself ... With
the kitsch-tropical décor of the natives' palm-wood gods hovering
goon-like around me in silent and haughty censure. (Smirking like
headmaster Arnold of old, damn his fat face! A hundred-and-fifty
years since expulsion from Rugby, can it really be?) With their deep-
set eyes crossed over their big, adze-shaped noses — drilling holes
into me as if to declare:

> Look, see that repatriated old corpse slumped gecko-eyed,
> cadging drinks on the corner stool there: his flesh dark-and-
> lined as if holed up in a copra smoke-house this past year ...
> That's Harry Paget Flashman VC. Knight of the Realm, can
> you believe? Old public school bovver-boy — wastrel,

coward, drunkard and scoundrel. Con-artist *sans pareil*, and fornicator supreme. Steer well clear of him!

And, eyeing my reflection in the bar mirror, I'm half-inclined to agree. What-ho Harry old son, I think: After all the grand-rattling adventures, scams, schemes, stunts and close scrapes — the years of heroic-scale whoring, and incomprehensible, scandalous rise through the ranks: has it *really* come to such? To be hobbled in the company of such folk as these, in such a place as this! Ears being equally chewed by hymn-singers and by glaze-eyed old bores near as bad as yourself. Awaiting the chance of another thin fleece, or to try it on with some desperate widow when the *Pacific Pearl* puts in for a day, on one of a half-dozen times each year ...

God's truth but it's queer to be me! If Life's just *half* the wild, roll-eyed mare, wet-ready-and-ripe for the taking, as I've always seen her to be — then she's kicked old Harry in the knap-sack most royally. With real vengeance, eh. And bolted right off, abandoned me here in the cruellest, most despicable way. Washed up alone, full of years, with my rotten teeth aching and an ailing prostate. Corralled in this cunnyless, coral-poxed place fit to bake my brains. And though there's champion irony (and undeniable symmetry) in the concept of a veteran schoolyard bully being bullied into Life's corner himself at the end of his days — still, it *hurts*! To be so brutally thrown for a jockey who's younger, fitter, abler and more to Life's favour over the jumps! Tossed arse-over-breakfast, cartwheeling to the ground — or onto a bar stool in a dingy hotel in Luganville. On Espiritu Santo: 'Isle of the Holy Spirit' so-called, damn the black, cankered heart of the place!

*   *   *

Yes. Harry's spirit is sorely ailing, God's truth ... And yet in all of it, there's this single queer thing: Sometimes, I swear, just now and then — ever since that mad-raving, moon-tupping Dark-Night-of-the-Harry-Soul last year, when I sent the VC and KCB skittering in a high, glittering arc out over the reef, to fumble the long-handled razor to my uptilted throat — just *sometimes*, I swear: there are mornings when my decrepit heart lifts, at sight of the pearl-like light on the lagoon. And I swoon like a gibbering virgin to see the barnstorming swallows swooping the hotel lawn, weaving gay lassos round the frangipanis and the Dragons Blood tree. When light winkles its way into my reptile-eye, and my weary heart trembles with hope: that the blood might yet make one last glorious stand in my shrunken thighs at the prompt of a prettily turned leg. Or my heartbeat skip at the scent of some dull poltroon screaming like a loon to be deliciously gulled — or at some other such-like champion scam or ruse ... And I think: the deuce, Harry! Keep faith, man! Live in hope! You never know, you silly old, oversmoked, sentimental, swollen-prostated son-of-a-whore — in between buying your coconut bread on tab at the Japanese bakery, and outfitting yourself with cast-offs from Bunny Fung's General Store — between cadging drinks, and having your ears chewed off by inveterate hotel bores — you just *might* turn one fine, final trick. Yes: one last glorious ruse, tumble or stunt, just *might* come stumbling its way into you, and set you up for your very best escapade yet!

Four times Webster: the words, the words!

James Murray, 1837–1915

If a cortex could ever be scarred, or scored
(raised in cicatrix-like whorls) by *words*,
then that cortex would have to have been his:
the man poised, gymnast lean-and-tall,
with forked-white, Elijah-like beard.
At the lectern-helm of his rickety ship,
the Scriptorium: contrived from iron sheets
in his Oxford backyard,
as halfway-house to the words
to be permanently housed in the Great Work.

Unfaltering in his belief of Providence guiding him,
of God lying deep-and-mysterious at the heart of words —
as, caught Laocoön-like in their grip,
he struggled year-upon-year.
Warring the Oxford Press delegates' budgets and schedules,
the incessant demands to rein the beast in.
And the vastly greater tribulations
of the lexicographical task itself.
        (The 16-column train-wreck of the word 'Set',
        and abomination of 'Put';
        the endless nightmare of the letter 'S'.
        The prevailing sense of general shortfall
        as he worked —
        and particular regret for no chance to redo
        the whole of the letter 'E' again) …
Flaying himself all this while with these Words, Words, Words.
Taking brief respite at the Welsh seaside
and with hikes in The Malverns.
Or with round-town rides aboard his velocipede —

pigeonholed as an entry for the letter 'V',
to which he never got: the 36 years of his life
gone into the great-inky sinkhole of the thing
only getting him to 'T' by its end.
Leaving 13 years more for his successor to complete the work,
with the initial contractual brief of keeping the project to '4 times
Webster'
blowing out to 12 volumes plus a one-volume Supplement.

Then, extraordinarily (See 'Sisyphean', "*adj.*:
an impossible task you can never complete"):
in process of the work being revised, expanded and digitised
for putting online in 1988,
the whole thing was letter-for-letter rekeyed.

      An inconceivable enough task for *us* to imagine.
      Indescribably more mind-boggling
      as it would have been for him.

Ode to Leo Fender (1909–1991)

We gather in praise of Leo:
tone-deaf non-muso
and Anaheim orange-orchardist's son —
Father of the Strat!

Which Keith raps for its essential lightness-of-being:
its contour design, hugging your body's coast-line
without dragging you down
so you can play all night without strain to shoulder or back.
'Kick of a mule, style and pace of a racehorse.'
The Big Boys Tool. The Ultimate Axe.

Praise Leo! Praise Leo! Hail the Strat!
Wire it up whichever way you want,
it's got everything needed for the job.
To trick the truest licks from your hand,
from mellow downstrokes and soft chops,
through funky jazz riff —
tremolo, echo, wah-wah —
or ramped all the way up
to 'blow-your-socks-off' grade feedback.
For which we praise Leo! — All hail the Strat!

For Eric, the Strat simply *is* rock-'n'-roll:
pure, vital and whole. It's sexy, and lustful —
a great white page upon which to write your electric-self,
with a lot of him already in it he found.
Hooked at first taste, he buried his Gibson and Gretsch
at the crossroads, never looked back.

Gloria, gloria in excelsis Leo!
First came the Telecaster, then the Broadcaster —

and then came the Strat!
Supreme workhorse. The only guitar in the shop!

Yes, it's not Clapton who's God, but the Strat!
Though some say that in *Jimi* the Strat met its full match.
Like the devil, he played it left-handed
        (a standard, right-handed model,
        flipped upside-down) —
but ditto could play with his teeth,
through his legs and behind his nape.
Riding the instrument bareback
through fire, smoke and ball-lightning:
        Whomp! VAMP! Kerrr-ZONK! …
        PHizzz. Kaah-SPLATTTT!!!
Pushing the thing to the edge of its electric envelope
before turning its Mothership safely for home …

Though, frankly, many were shocked
when he smashed his Strat up
like a chair in a barroom-brawl
on the stage floor at Monterey Pop.
Knelt to baptise it with squirts of butane
and then set it alight.

'To smash up a Strat!' Keith reportedly gasped,
'I'd rather cut someone's throat than do that,
it's like deliberately stacking your Rolls!'
And the Fender Company, likewise:
'I know he's now dead,' its MD years later said —
'but I'll never forgive that young fellow!'
(Though, in the wicked, wily, sex-drugs & rock-'n'-roll
way of this world,
sales had gone right through the roof after that.)

And so, for a host of rock luminaries,
the Strat's ever remained the instrument of choice.
>   (For both of the Buddys — Guy, and Holly —
>   for Harrison, Lennon … Beck, Cooder, Knopfler,
>   Robertson, Raitt —
>   Pete Townshend, The Edge and Stevie Ray Vaughan,
>   to name some.)

And so the Strat rocks today, these more than 60 years on:

>   *For which we praise Leo, Leo, Leo!*
>   *Tone-deaf non-muso guitar-maker genius.*
>   *Inductee of the Rock 'n' Roll Hall of Fame.*
>   *Luthier-legend sans pareil —*
>   *Father of the Strat!*

Accountants at war

630 members of the Australian Institute of Chartered Accountants served in World War Two. At least 40 were killed. Most saw little, or gave scant thought to, Accountancy during the six-year conflict. Meetings with fellow-accountants were haphazard and rare.

At conflict's end — as was the case for veterans of all the other professions — some accountants found difficulty resuming their pre-war lives. Suffering badly frayed nerves, panic attacks on buses and trams; an array of disorders and traumas of varying degrees and kinds.

More fortuitously, some accountants had found that their training helped sustain them through the war years. Chip Johnson, a 17-year-old seaman on HMAS *Perth* (sunk in Sunda Strait in March 1942) survived three years in a Japanese prison camp on 90 grams of rice a day — and helped maintain camp morale teaching bookkeeping to fellow inmates. (National President of the Ex-POW Association today, he's been an Accountancy Institute member since 1949.)

Australia post-war faced substantial challenges, with the changed financial laws and tax measures applicable for return to the peacetime economy. With professional supply unable to meet demand, Accountancy study was encouraged for ex-service personnel. Over 1600 veteran candidates sat the Institute's first-round exams.

The Accountancy profession served with distinction in this new space — helping preserve the integrity of the numbers, and keep the nation's books straight.

Relieving the camp

When Rainbow Division reached the camp, they found the
administration had fled,
along with most of the guards — barring a garland of diehard SS
holding out in the towers.
Screaming abuse down upon the inmates' heads
to the living end.

Regular German battlefield troops had been assigned for the camp's
surrender,
so it was these who brunted the GIs' confusion and rage ...
And it's true the takeover was an untidy affair.
Brutal, unsoldierly, unprofessional. Certainly not done by the rules.
But in retrospect, perhaps a natural enough response
to the unusual situation too: with the battle-weary troops
pressing hard on the German retreat to Munich,
blundering into it all unprepared. (Unpreparable, in truth.)
The rail-yard lighting their way in —
2000 skeletal cadavers abandoned in open boxcars
and strewn like refuse all about,
many with bullet-holes to the back of the head ...

Then arriving at the camp-gate itself,
and the wraiths hovering behind the wire.
In face of which some GIs seemed paralysed
by pure incredulousness. Some openly wept,
as the striped pyjamas — stupefied likewise,
thin-gruel smiles, great luminous eyes,
scarecrow faces cropped with sores —
gaped meanwhile back through the wire at them.
Before letting slide strangled cheers, or dancing feeble jigs.
Some dropped to their knees, others stood quietly hugging
and rocking themselves,

gently swayed and prayed with bowed, shaven heads ...
Each GI and prisoner equally finding their own private
and personal means of release.
In that place which, my Christ,
was one of the innermost circles of hell ...

Then slowly the prisoners came more certainly
into themselves. Something stirred,
a subtle shift rippling over parts of the yard
as some of the inmates rounded on others,
setting upon them with boots and fists.
There's a report of GIs outside the wire
being prevailed upon to nudge a guard in
through the gates to them; then turn a blind eye
as the inmates railed upon this titbit.
Kicking, and beating. Flailing at the man like a *piñata*,
competing to tear off the head;
to dance upon him in their pure exaltation
and impossible deliverance.
There in Death's spare, filthy, grey-shitting yard.
In this suburb a 20-minute tram-ride from downtown Munich.

There are reports likewise of guards being bundled
into bunker blocks and savagely dealt with.
Thrown up against the nearest wall and summarily shot,
their bodies lumped into the adjacent canal.
And one report of a mass execution of guards by Browning
machinegun
in the camp barracks next door ...

We are yet to investigate these matters to their core.
But off the record (and to cite the words of one NCO
as reported back to me):
In the fuller context of the thing — though such acts
were clear violations, contrary to rule-of-law,

and not sanctionable in the end —
might they not also be seen in some basic sense
as a pure-and-naked human response
to the terrible situation there?
Understandable in part, at least?

And, in all truth could you deny
that if you had come on that place,
you too might have turned your eye away
to let the scene unfold.
Or — at a dark stretch, taken by some dark,
private impulse of your own —
have participated in such acts yourself?

Law & order: legally blind

They said that I wasn't legally blind:
I was only a probationer,
and to qualify and be fully rated
I'd need to get more experience under my belt —
then officially pass the test.

It was a serious offence, till then,
to impersonate blindness they said.
I'd been had for trying it on twice before
and the new, low-tolerance regime
was losing patience with me now …

If they catch me trying it on again,
it's three strikes and I'm out:
they'll settle the matter permanently,
and put both my eyes out themselves —
for good.

'A constellation of abnormalities'

His cardiologist proves unexpectedly foxy: scalpel-sharp makeup around the eyes; sassy, blonde bouffe. Flashy, floor-clacking heels under a short, lollipop-stripe, pleated skirt. And she looks remarkably fit — like she runs ...

And as she's sat perusing his charts, he imagines her jogging the sands of her holiday beach-house, on one of those remoter stretches of coast where the whales incline to beach themselves. Appearing suddenly at the crest of a dune sprawled with lush-pink pigface. Pausing momently in her dove-grey, designer track-suit, before coursing down and on; sand flicking up from her neat-kicking Reeboks' heels. Meticulously pacing herself as she goes: every bit as wonderfully cognisant and comfortable as you'd expect with the intimate-and-intricate working of her own beating heart ... But she breaks these foolish fantasies by suddenly hauling up straight over his spreadeagled printouts, and in a casual, almost teasing way (as if they're chatting on cocktail barstools almost), surmise the results:

'A constellation of abnormalities,' she cheerily states. At first he thinks he's not heard her straight — but she says it again. Showing disconcertingly little concern for her words' impact; evidently amused with her turn-of-phrase.

'Christ, where'd she get *that* from?' he thinks to himself: Is it something classical (Aristotle? The Book of Ezekiel? St John of the Cross?) Straight from the mouth of the original-and-great heart-man Harvey himself: freshly twigged to the blood-flow principle and mechanical essence of the heart-as-pump? Might it be something mathematical (Heisenberg's Uncertainty Principle, or such?) Or some contemporary, in-house shorthand freely bandied about at medical conferences these days: as professional 'get-out-of-jail' card, or Medispeak-style brush-off.

(Equivalent of 'the cheque's in the mail'; subtext 'What-the-cardiological-*fuck*!?') … Any or none of these, who could say?

Or finally, might the lady have minted the phrase herself? And why not? Should 25 years' intense medical training preclude you from being a poet as well? At heart. It would be pure arrogance to deny her the right to such.

Yes. Well, *anyway*: 'a constellation of abnormalities' is what came out. Tossed off by her with a whimsical nod. And the gentlest of beguiling frowns with just a twist of surprise in it: as if she'd looked up at her drug-company desk-clock to realise how late in the day it had suddenly got. And that she'll need to kick this consultation along — get her cardiological skates on — if she wants time to get home to tug on her Lorna Jane sports shorts and top and fit in her evening jog.

Patriarch: the King of Sardinia

Men's Ward, Calvary Hospital

Act 1: The king

Plumped on his haughty-high pillows
he surveys his domain with a despot's eye
as he ponderously talks and gesticulates,
the saline-drip trembling with each move of his mottled, right hand.
And his family fawns silent and abject bedside,
as if taking dictation in their heads.

At 84, he's been brought here following a night-time fall;
allegedly suffering breathlessness.
But for that he could talk all the rest of us
      (me with my pulmonary embolism,
      the bloke-with-the-stroke,
      the fisherman with liver nodules,
      and the ex-RAN diver lost half a lung
      through his dive-team's negligence)
the proverbial six feet underground.
Then dance the Ballu Sarda on top of us, as well.

Yes, ninety per cent of the ward's noise is him, for sure.
Jabbering away, words running down over his grizzled jaw
and his open, striped-cotton pyjamas
to pool in the mess of his big, grey-matted chest.
And when his family's skived off for some R&R
after having their ears chewed off,
he's working the bedside phone.
Got the thing clasped two-handed in a tennis pro's
smash backhand, busy menacing someone else.
Gabbling his ceaseless Sardinian,

till the sardines must be beaching themselves,
ears bleeding, upon half the beaches of this earth.
(How can one 84-year-old man
have so much left to say, with such passion and urgency,
to the rest of the world?)
And if that somehow all miraculously, momently, stops,
he's running the nurses ragged with queries, decrees or commands,
sopping attention up like a surgical sponge.

Now, while this might be diverting up to a point, for some,
the man's wildly exceeded that.
He's a terrorist, who needs to be taken down.
A great, wheezing black-hole, sucking entire nurse-stations
cartwheeling backwards, flailing head-over-tail,
to extinguish themselves in him.
Leaving the rest of us all essentially marooned,
to forage for ourselves.

Act 2: The hitchhiker — a farewell performance

On the morning he's scheduled for home,
he drops his pyjama shorts to the floor
to stand like a lap-dancer, twisting and angling himself,
to exhibit the bruise set like a beetroot spill on his thigh.
As his penis protrudes in profile
from the broken nest of his pitted groin:
like an ancient thumb hitching a ride
back down the road to the days of his youth.
The time when he'd just arrived as a buck immigrant,
with Australia primed to fall to him
in some kind of *droit de signor*;
to be done with by him as he would.

As he's stood in his jagged breath,
gazing down pondering himself:
like there's 84 years more,
idling there in his ricotta-white, varicosed thigh,
and the blasted mare's-nest of his barrel-chest.
And he could shuck all the decades off in a stride
and redeliver himself to 1952.
Sign up for the job again right now,
do the whole thing over once more.

But he tugs up his shorts instead.
Limps to his bedside cabinet, and commences to slowly dress.
Then plumps himself quietly to wait on the end of his bed,
for his son to come and collect him and bear him home.

Induced-birth method

Kibbutz Ginegar, Jezreel Valley, Israel, 1978

Aaron leaps from his battered Ferguson,
in his army boots and boiler-suit,
clutching a short length of rope
like the Boston Strangler's pantyhose —
as he leads me to the back end of the cow.
At which we crouch. Reefing a leather work-glove off,
he inserts a big fat dipstick finger. Probes,
then paws the slobbering slit-purse apart
to disclose the calf. Packed in there tight as the second-row:
>two shy feet put tremblingly forward,
>stepping-stones to the outside world.
>Pink wedge of tongue-and-snout.
>One slippery-lidded, blue-blond eye
>ogling groggily out.

He scratches his cheek, lights up a cigarette, inhales.
Considering the lay of this — then snatches up the rope,
slip-knots a tie around the hooves, thrusts one end at me, and croaks:
>'When I say so, we pull. *Straight out,*
>not down, or else we kill them both.'

We each gather our slack, and brace. He nods, we tug —
at first to no avail: the cow holds firm,
as if considering her inclination or her rights.
Cow's and calf's alien joint-life
straining huge and taut — kite-like,
and strangely ominous — within my hands.
As if the cow was booby-trapped;
its belly packed with dynamite.

A pause. Then we both tug hard again,
and the cow caves in this time. Relents — jolts forward
and relinquishes her load: slip-sliding in one great-blind,
racing gush the calf erupts like a self-inflating rubber dinghy.
So suddenly and tumultuously there
        (dumped slick-wet, live, whole and legless —
        half-nelsoned to the ground, inhaling dust)
that I want to laugh in wonderment, almost … But don't.

As the cow, unburdened now, steps free of her lasso-hoop
of umbilical and steaming afterbirth —
yawls round to dip her big head down,
stands snuffling over her cooked load.
When Aaron cuts the cord, she sidles out her long blue tongue
to lick off the silky, gummy web of luminous meniscus —
then bellows, suddenly — startlingly loud —
and nudges this sly, soft-rude mess
and heap of lazybones
to unpack its thin, card-table legs, and stand.
But Aaron heads this off, shoulders in to snatch the bundle up
and totes it like a long, square washing-load in both big arms.
Berths it in the tractor's bucket-maw, then leaps himself aboard.
Tosses me a wave, and guns off in a snort of diesel smoke.

The cow stands silent, listing dumbly forward then.
Staring at the barn's far wall. With eggy eyes,
small coronet of horns. Absorbing this sideswipe:
this impulse (life) been bodily hijacked from her.
Then dips her head again, to snuffle the gored straw.

I reach out to touch her oblong flank:
massive as an old barn-door, but trembling, damp and warm.
As she's standing there, four-square. Bereft.
In the mucous mess of scattered straw, and perfunctory obstetrics
of Ginegar's hard calving-yard.

Bounty-hunters: picking mushrooms in rain

Combe Martin, North Devon, 1977
for Sal

We stumble on their wild, abundant accident:
bursting head-up from the ground,
offering themselves in the field;
blooming in light-falling rain.

Each head feeling tender, full, soft and round
to the stroke as a cat's purring jowls
as we squat and plunder them:
inclining itself singly up
as we snap it cleanly off at its stalk
to topple its ticklish weight
into our cupped hand ...

When we've taken enough
you strip your scarf off
and lay it on the ground. And we fill it up
with an abundance of mushrooms.
Then, tying it in a loose knot,
I slip this scarf-bundle inside my jacket front.
Zip it up. And, pregnant with their gentle, slain weight,
and being careful not to slip on the wet track,
we walk back down the hill together into town.
Moving like bounty-hunters through the light-falling rain.

*   *   *

After towelling our hair dry in the kitchen,
you teach me how to fry the mushrooms up

in a sizzling lasso of butter and black pepper,
in a pan set on a low flame ...
Then slip a fork into one, and tip it to my mouth.
To taste:

these mushrooms —
golden-brown titbits of untamed vegetable-stuff,
taken from the dark hills of the combe.
This small, North Devon village's big game.

Conservation

I set fire to a chimney in my aunt's hotel,
the 'Pack O' Cards' Inn
(a 'Grade II Ancient Monument'
under Britain's *Statutory List of Buildings*
of Special Architectural Interest),
in a North Devon village near Ilfracombe once,
in 1978.

It was 287 years old at the time
(I'd just seen my twenty-third birthday) —
and built by a local squire from cob-&-stone,
in the shape of a house-of-cards,
to commemorate a gaming win.
And I ran up its four floors
(one representing each card suit),
trailing a garden hose —
passing en route through the requisite number
of the building's 13 doors-&-rooms
(one for the number of cards in each suit):
breathing hard all the way up the 52 stairs,
to open a window at the top.
Which was fitted with one of the building's
52 panes of glass
(that is, at least, before the window tax).
To give shout to my cousin below
to turn on the garden tap …
Then stepped out onto the bituminised balcony-roof
to shove the hose-nozzle hard
into the billowing chimney cap.

I was gambling on this putting the fire out,
which thank Christ it did.
And so the Pack O' Cards still stands today,
in its gleaming, white-washed, heritage cob-&-stone.
325 years old as I write.

The 'Little Mermaid': a defence

Langelinie, Copenhagen Harbour

The Little Mermaid's missing from her post — Again.
Considered as fair laughing stock
and fit object for contempt, by some,
she suffers serially at their hands.
Routinely abducted and graffitied
(decapitated even, once)
in the continual struggle to survive
in her hard place on the rock.

Yet, like the legend from which she's spun, she prevails,
with the industrial-grade strength of all fairytales.
Retrieved from ditch, canal — parking lot or student squat —
to be mended, cleaned, and faithfully cemented
back into her spot …

I saw her here seven years ago:
       soft-dipping shoulder, shy puppy breasts,
       wet tresses clinging to her heart-shaped face;
       peering tamely down into the seawater
       from which we all came.
And kitsch she seemed, quite certainly —
but strangely heroic too, somehow,
in her determinedness to stake her place.
She had resonance of a kind:
tenderly dug herself in, taking her radical strain
against the brash world.

And so, though absent again today,
you don't doubt she'll be back.
That Little Mermaid is bulletproof. Failsafe.
There for all time. For good, and for us.

Towards the words

1 The editor's plaint

'Publishing houses are increasingly bypassing editorial processes to reduce costs'

There were Editors once, who wandered this Earth,
though the people threw up their hands and protested
at the butchering of all their 'precious, hard-earned words'.
Still, the editors hardened their hearts:
held the line, and held their nerve.
And with more determined grip of their pens
persevered in wading the texts.
Honed, cut, shaped — checked facts,
made substitute of an ill-judged phrase or word.
Revised each manuscript till it hurt
before seamlessly sewing it up again.

They returned to the fray, day-after-day,
though at undoubted cost to their psychological health.
Though at every page-turn, just as one fault in the MS
was subdued (tamed or contained),
some new barbarism would erupt
to strike fresh fear in a reader's heart;
impale itself upon a fresh page.

They battled on — even though as one MS was saved,
a thousand more botched ones tumbled bleeding,
squawking and flapping to earth.
And the whole process saw no permanent advance,
with nothing much ever seeming to be learned.
And the editor's craft remained forever suspect,
their intent forever misconstrued,
and the remuneration paltry and absurd.

And though, as often as not,
for all their lavish attention and devotion,
upon publication they would hardly even be thanked ...

There were Editors once, who wandered this Earth.

2 Paper-cut ('Accident on the A4')

This empty sheet of paper
is a high-precision tool
and potentially dangerous instrument,
demanding absolute respect.
Look now! See how, in being reckless —
rushing in with your dull pen,
so cavalier in what you wrote:
your dullard hand has slipped, you fool!
You bleed. You've cut yourself!

3 Party time

Words are wary strangers
come to party in a paper room.
Needing time to feel each other out,
and come on slowly to each other
and themselves.

Some quite quickly give it up,
slip resignedly away.
Some get bodily thrown out.
While others may gatecrash events unasked.

Eventually, you'll find some left,
standing in a natural group,
each with a friendly drink in hand
and quietly enjoying themselves.
As each contributes their essential part
to a vital conversation.

4 Romancing the poem

Circling the heap of words
sprawled upon the ground,
you nudge them with the toe of your work boot.
Contrive to have them move —
assume some meaning; shape.

Offer them the simple choice
of either staying down —
rolling over there and then,
to die right where they lie…

or struggle to their feet,
and come out fighting for themselves.
To find their own true voice.

5 The edit

If you can take out a word
with no arguable loss:
there's in fact
an inarguable gain.

Three views to a hippopotamus

1
A hippo walks out of the river
like a couch out of a car-wash ...

2
It is: the log that badly jammed the mill ...
The square peg hammered into
the round hole.

3
Or, if we can really believe the name
is ancient Greek for 'river horse' —
then the Greeks got either their 'river' or 'horse' badly wrong.

It is a 'horse' of profoundly problematic kind:

>   a Thoroughbred foal held captive
>   ten years in a cellar —
>   force-fed cheeseburgers, till its teeth fall out
>   and it's gone half-blind.

>   The absolute toxic nadir
>   of the equine breeding line:
>   (Phar Lap out of Bhopal;
>   Black Caviar out of Minamata).

It is: the poor, pink, naked, howling creature
branded on forehead, and set afire —
sent toppling, kicking-and-flailing from Heaven
to be permanently put from divine sight-&-mind.

The bath

is a sleek, enamel-skinned machine
in which you steep yourself each evening,
attired in your nude-suit.
(Flying solo, in the usual case.)
Gripping the rails, strapped in at the hips,
with both feet pointed forward to steer —

then, adjusting the throttles
of the hot-&-cold taps
to fine-tune the cabin temperature,
you lean back to edge both shoulders in —
and slip the thing into gear ...

Or:

It's an incubator
which helps you read, think (or sleep).
It eases the muscles, salves the nerves, loosens cramps.
If required, it will faithfully monitor your heartbeat.

It is your delicious, liquescent Field-of-Dreams,
the soft-focus place set on the steamy-tropical
periphery of things:
to melt away vicissitudes
and help assuage Life's tedium,
transgressions or regrets ...

as all the while it gently plays (diverts itself)
with little, odd bits of you
which float-and-bob about
according to your body type and sex.

Russian doll: an unsolicited email

'Increasing numbers of women from the old USSR are seeking male partners
in the west' — *newspaper report*

'Ukraine girls really knock me out' — *John Lennon*

Hello my friends! You know just now Lubow is wondering
why she is not hear from you. (Is cold in Kiev,
she needs her mens to keep her warm!)
And then she finds your last emails
hiding in her spam filters (You shy-boys you!)
So writes again remind you of her facts:

> Ages: 26. Hair: blonds. Weights: 60 kilograms.
> As please can see photos attach.
> Good sense of humours, easy-going down
> to earths, and living here in Kiev-Ukraine
> with my only mum. I have my own apartments dears!
> And work as dance teachers,
> to keep me beautiful-and-fits. (Good moneys too! ☺)

So, maybe you are think: Well this Lubow is having everythings
to living her whole happy lives — But No!
She cannot find her own true loves and Love-of-All-My-Lifes!
(Good mens already married sad but true.)
And so is look in internets to help to meet her special ones,
and thinking that is maybe you!!!

But listen first, to telling two importants things:
1. Lubow is genuine GOOD womens,
   not low-down dirty partys-girl.
   She does not ask for moneys help.
2. Also is need SINCERE relationships.

With many loves to give her mens
who are loving Lubow very big also!

So anyways — I wish you lovely days my friends!
Do svidaniya dears, for now. But don't forget your sweet Lubow
who wants to be your very best girlfriends (not just penpals).
And remembering her home emails:
Kiev-woman1@hotmail.com
for speakings to your Ukraine-girls soon please!

Activity: Sally-Jane

Sally-Jane's just jetted in from Paris. She's sitting in her fave Crown Street cafe.

The whole gang knows her, sipping their short blacks and capps, their mochas and lattés. She's joking with her favourite waiter. Smiling casual g'days — tilts her handsome hair right back, to laugh her big, red-firebucket lipstick at the ceiling.

Sal's cool. She's awesome. At 16 she left school to get into the band scene: 'Late nights playing clubs and dives. Talent is God-given, but then it's up to you. If you work real hard, maintain the proper attitude, the sky's the limit!'

You'd say that Sal was confident. Passionate. Determined: 'I always hogged the spotlight eh. A real live-wire party girl, even as a toddler. Getting up to dance on tables at all my parents' parties. You'd say I'm pretty "in-your-face". And if there's something that I want — then watch out mate, I'll get it!'

The waiter sashays by again, leans close to whisper into Sally's ear. Sal pulls back and snorts: 'Geez Damian, get a life won't you!' Dames pouts, reaches out to confiscate her coffee cup, minces on his way. 'Hey Damian,' Sal cries, 'I haven't finished that cup yet mate! What's got into you!'

ACTIVITIES

Splitting into groups, discuss:

1. Does Sally-Jane like her career? Would you say that she was 'born to it'?
2. Do you think Sal's got life fully sussed? Or could there be more to it?
3. Read back through paragraph four again.
   a) Why should Damien 'get a life'?
   b) How might he commence to do it?

Safe at any speed: horse on the Hume Motorway

Driving home from Sydney,
after passing the naff, orange-pole sculpture
at the Light Horse Interchange,
I'll typically fall my car in behind
the first truck I find in the far left lane.
Set cruise control, and surf in its wake ...
Letting everything else hurtle madly by
perpetually overtaking itself to my right,
as I skive off some private thinking-space for myself.

But *this* day a horse-float, drawn by a Range Rover,
glides in from the Campbelltown feeder-lane:
the animal's tail slung over the trailer's back,
a thick, black flag emphatically planted in my face
to contemplate — which I do.
Amusing myself with thought of a horse
doing 100 kay without taking its coat off
or raising a sweat ...

And, as another overpass flicker-folds over us
in this staggered steeplechase,
I wonder what a horse might think while travelling a motorway:
with the long, straight stretch of bitumen-and-concrete
passing existentially under-wheel
like an alien-and-hostile turf;
the scent of paddocks and hills rolling by just out of reach ...
Would it suffer freeway ennui, like myself?
Get stressed if some other piece of horse-flesh
sailed blithely by in a faster float, overtaking it?
Or feel secure enough in its own mature, horsey sense-of-self
(trajectory through time and space)
to continue to run its own race?

The horse and I both take the Berrima turnoff —
canter the rise, to carousel the roundabout
as the great stampede of the motorway drops off behind.
I pull in at the park with its big, dark, heritage pines —
but the horse courses on, in its wheeled box:
trundled on past the alpaca wool-shop
and the old sandstock White Horse Inn
(in scaffold, and up for sale again) ...

Being tenderly freighted on through this world —
as I sit with my thermos coffee and cake
and am freighted on through mine.

Parents & citizens: nesting season, Armidale

His daughter is toddling towards him
as it swoops out of the ribbon gum, and sun —
and he parries the shovel in a baseball stroke:
just managing to clip the bird, which crumples to the ground —
recovers — reasserts itself, in a feisty little break-dance.
Then hobbles off scowling, sideways:
one wing hung awrily down; a crack-head's burned-out eyes.
'*Bir*! *Bir*!' his daughter points in pure astonishment,
fitting this late-learned word to the world.
As he jams his shovel into the earth,
steps across and hauls her to her feet,
then gathers her higher into his arms.
Turns to the bird, and states:

> 'You look to your young, Mr Bird, I guess.
> And I will look to mine.'

The editor's wife: a letter. (Reprise)

for their 25th

If you came in to meet me at town hall station,
we could see a movie perhaps.
You'd kick off your shoes, to sit cross-legged
in your seat, hands folded in your lap.
As I sneaked tantalised, sidewards looks at you:
floored by your body's sense-of-ease.

I'd buy us both Choc-Tops at interval
(you'd ask to pay for yours; I'd chivalrously decline).
Then we'd go on to a Lebanese restaurant,
and I'd duck across Cleveland Street in the rain
for a bottle of the Wyndham Estate cab-sav that we both like.

If we then went back to your Wigram Road terrace,
you could invite me in. Slip *Kind of Blue* onto the stereo,
and we'd drink jasmine tea, and talk —
so I'd learn that after a two-year stint in Moree
and six months at a Baulkham Hills school down here,
you were burned right out from teaching.
          (Nine-parts playing policeman, one-part just trying
          to keep the kids half-interested, as you said.)
And we'd scheme ways to give you a break.

Then, six months later, you'd move into my Newton flat with me...
And taking a ten-year leap on from that
(with you having returned to teaching again)
you and our two girls would be catching the train
back to our Canberra home
from a school holiday break on the coast.
(I would bring you your coats to the station,

on account of the sudden cold snap up here.)

But with this we'd be getting far ahead of ourselves —
for at the point at which I am speaking now,
we have barely met. I've just finished the page-proofs
of this wretched freelance job, after working twelve hours straight.
And am just taking a moment to send this email:
to suggest that we meet for a movie in town
one evening this week, if it fits … And await your response,
poised here, at the possible, perilous flowering
of this extraordinary, delicate thing.

And it would be a very great stretch — a conceit,
presumptuous to the highest degree —
to see you as the Editor's Wife as yet.

The slippery sky: AF 447, June 2009

Hearing news of the Air France Airbus
inexplicably tumbling from the night sky
into the sea off Brazil —
we lament the loss of the three Dublin women medical graduates
extinguished at the start of their promising careers;
the 10 French factory employees and spouses
returning from their performance-reward holiday;
the 11-year-old boy, en route to commence
the new term at his Bristol boarding school ...
And the 204 others — passengers and crew —
who were lost in the incident too.
All each, in their way, held equally close and dear.

> And for a week or two (or perhaps for some months)
> we all fly in a little more fear.

Little Sisters of Mercy (The laying out)

'Clear off!' the old man had bawled to the Sisters
on their rounds the night before:
'Just bugger off, Sweet Christ can't you,
and leave me alone!'

But the Little Sisters of Mercy couldn't.
(Can't ... Won't.)
The man dies in the night, and by soft morning light
the Little Sisters return:
to clean him, and dress him, and lay him out
in the manner they might suppose he'd like, or choose.

Comb out his lank beard and hair,
bending over him as they gently work.
Slowly mothering him to death.

Then wheel him in to another, colder room,
stretchered upon a gurney.
Laid like a terrible baby
in its terrible, last, sad bassinette.

The House of Dementia

1 The ward

We're invading their space — and they behave
as they naturally would: Confused.
Asking whether we're staff.
Have we seen their husband in the corridor?
Or can we show them, please, which is their room?

One, with crystal-cut voice — a hospital matron
in Burma in World War II:
and just had her walking-frame confiscated
because of repeated falls —
has commandeered a dining-room chair
which she bangs jackhammer-like round the hall.

Another sits thumbing a salt-cellar two-handed,
like a gameboy. And one creeps into the others' night rooms
to shake them awake at 2, 3 or 4,
then apologise and pad away in her elfin slippers.
In her endless roll-call: ensuring that all
are present-and-accounted-for.
Here, in the House of Dementia.

Here in the Dementia Ward —
where each is explorer of their own interior, alien,
ever-changing, unchanging realm.
And where sometimes, if you take their hand,
their face might suddenly bloom like a camellia,
in soft remembrance of something.
Or instead, their eyes might stare hard as a freight train
crashing straight through you —
on account of their feeling unaccountably ragged or angry,

or indefinably out-of-sorts
on some matter they're disinclined to discuss
(or at least discuss with *you*).
Or because they simply can't be sure
how precisely they might be inclined to feel today, at all ...

Here, where life can get terribly lost, tender and bruised.
As they wonder why this great ship-of-a-place
can't be pointed about, and put on its proper course;
if they could just manage to work that out.
As it all taunts them, floating there.
In the clear, lucid space they can sometimes sense
beating thick, warm and close
as a planted kiss at their jugular...
Skin-deep, through the pink-pastel wall.

2 'You live here now': a drama

Scene 1.

Nurse: Where do you want to go, Alfred?
Alfred *(Stops, and turns. Tentatively)*: Can I ... Go ... *Home?*
Nurse: You *are* home, Alfred ... *This* is your home now.
(Alfred slowly sits, confused.)

Scene 2 (CHORUS):

— I don't know where I am ... I can't find my room!
— Where's my cup of tea? You can't even get a rotten cup of tea in the
place!
— I can't abide *uppity folk*. Or ones who get *angry*. (*Not mentioning
any names!*)

— Excuse me: Has anyone seen my *handbag*?

— Staff! *Staff!* Where are the *staff*!?... I want to talk to that nice young man!

— You *are* home, Alfred. You *are* home, dear ... You *live here* now.

They are home. They are home.
They are all home now. They are living here — Now.
In this big, pink-walled, white-carpeted Casa-of-the-Confused.
In the House of Dementia.

Intimacies: the gifts

The last gift
we give you
is the one that you really want:
to allow you to die.

And the last gift
you give *us* ...
is to allow us
to watch as you go.

Father & son

Lake Alexandrina, Murray Mouth, South Australia

The sudden storm upended them:
snapping their catamaran in two
like a communion wafer to some darkwater god,
tipping father-and-son into the lake's chill mass ...

Lifejackets coupled, they'd drifted then:
buoying themselves with talk,
the son feeding the father remembered stories from childhood,
to keep him awake and alert —

as the lake's cold fingers felt them up, all night.
And they threw occasional feeble strokes at the distant lights,
treading the endless, dark wheel to dawn:

when the son dragged the unconscious father ashore
to lay him on his side — then staggered off
through the reeds' maze for help.

But he'd died by the time it arrived.
The big lake that scuttles and drowns the great river
had shocked, and stopped, the father's heart. Silted it up.
And as the helicopter strapped the father's body aboard,
the son poured his grief out on the empty shore.

Three songs

1 The reservoir, the rituals

A man goes out fishing on the reservoir one day —
meets a storm, and doesn't come back.

Thus, each in their due capacity —
according to context (incidental, familial),
their professional calling or trade —
absorbs the impact. And enacts their part:

> the boy finds the overturned tinnie
> washed up on the shore;
> the police drag the reservoir floor;
> the family gathers to mourn;
> the funeral director and priest
> respectively minister the corpse.

As the rest of us all continue — incorrigibly, insatiably,
daily — to drink the same water from the tap.

2 The thing that dances on the hill

In the days of your youth,
Death is some mad, capricious creature
which dances abstractly on a distant rise.
Blurred; peripheral. Glimpsed sidewards, as it carousels
on its high hilltop while you drive through.
(Like that big, dramatic dead eucalypt stood in the paddock
on the Hume Highway at the Boorowa turn.)

You expend a great time ignoring it.
Can hardly conceive its temerity
to reach out and brazenly touch you.
Yes — though everything always indicates such,
you can't quite credit the pure audacity of Death
to come gunning personally for you.

Still, as you press more deeply into this life
the misconception's readily cured:
the understanding grows easier,
as Death edges itself consummately closer —
infiltrates family, friends and acquaintances
to get nearer to laying its breath on you.
And you realise ever more clearly, profoundly:
that Death intractably will.

3 'If Death had no Dominion': a burlesque

Funerals should run like weddings:
with that embedded wild card
(come 'get-out' clause)
of anyone being there-present
knowing of 'any legal impediment'
speaking up, to plead their cause.
Cobbling what excuses they might
        (the deceased being 'too young', or 'too good';
        the children left behind;
        the partner's incapacity to continue alone, and such like) —
so that Death might be ruled out-of-law.

Then the goon-suited funeral staff
would be obliged to stand down,
sidling awkwardly off to grab a quick smoke
alongside their redundant funeral cars.

As a family member gave thanks to all,
and apology for any inconvenience caused.

And the deceased, meanwhile,
scrambled like a newborn deer to their feet,
could gather and tidy themselves
for the whole family to head off for fish-&-chips
with the bleating, skip-footed gulls on the beach.

Before resuming the vital business of Life itself.
Determined to keep things more tight, this time:
show more diligence, care, application and purpose.
Seriousness-of-intent …

And so Death might have no dominion:
this one fine, sunny-bright day at least, yes?

After *Stormboy*: the Coorong, a lament

Younghusband Peninsula

Coorong what a fright you were:
shrunk to a crusty, linoleum sheen
of scaly blue-green. Reek like a rotted, beached whale.
We passed on your bird-hide, noses pressed into
our upturned shirts. Kept driving west, with the windows wound
tight ...
Till bailed up by a pelican in the middle of the road.

Climbing out, we herded the thing safe to the side,
where it stood unsteady on its great, flanged feet.
Reeling like a gagged hostage, with its pale beak wrapped
in a tangled mesh of spider web
thick as chain-mail before its crossed eyes.
Yawping in feeble defence of itself,
it tried hot-footing it off; wings gaping wide.
But we came in on the bird from four sides,
corralling it up between ourselves.
Used a stick to unpick the web's filthy-grey fairy-floss ...
Then left the thing to totter its way off.
Uncertain whether it'd survive the night:
bewitched, bothered, bewildered. Disenfranchised.
Palely loitering the scabby sedgeside.

We abandoned the pelican and Coorong both,
to sniff at the sore, skanky length of themselves
in the waning daylight.
Wondering where *Stormboy* had derailed,
as we left that place — waiting for rain,
for tide or river to turn, or for whatever might
cut this bastard knot and set things right.

To allow the Coorong to replenish itself, and run free again.
For the bird, with its great, unwieldy beak and big, saintly head,
to scamper-dance on its lumpen feet
and lurch itself into the air ...
Wheeling out over gleaming, fish-teeming waters.
Hurling itself back into the big, crooked-bright sky.

Island fling

Kangaroo Island

1 *Prologue*

At Penneshaw, suddenly things swing round.
The centre cannot hold:
and staring across 'The Passage', back to Port Jervois,
the mainland has become the island —
with the whole of the South Australian coast
shrunk to a long, curved bow.
And us on *this* side of the matter now ...

And for a week, the island is *it*:
as we kick up our heels, and rumble long, dusty hoops
on its empty, red-dirt roads ...
Led on in a fete of ivory lighthouses,
turquoise-blue water, flour-white beaches,
golden headlands and cays.
Reeling giddy at the edge of the sheer limestone cliffs,
and the tilting champagne light glancing off the sea ...

> With the seal and the sea-lion colonies
> incontestable star-acts of the show.

2 Motherlode

Seal Bay

In evolutionary terms, sea lions are related to bears —
but to me they are dogs, writ wrong:
with Evolution still got its work cut out

overhauling flank and chest —
redistributing the muscle mass, trimming excess weight ...
engineering flippers to forelegs and paws.
Fine-tuning the bark. Then rotating the hip
to give the creature the wherewithal
to rear upon its hind legs —
and by the scruff of its fat, sealy neck
be hauled permanently onto dry land.

       (Though that said, the effect of the bright spaniel-eyes
       is already surprisingly good.)

Barred from the house till then, the sea lions inhabit the fringes:
flounder in backyard sea-swells,
hobble-stomp shingle and sand —
or bask on the big, pumpkin-coloured rocks hereabouts.

*   *   *

But hey, look! Here's life!
A giddy yelp, as a pup explodes from the dunes
to come schmoodling itself roly-poly down.
Galumphing on towards Mum,
wobbling in, snout up, from the surf:
sleek, beige-silver and glistening,
swum her way back in over the girdling reef
from her three-days hunt, 70 kilometres out.
Slipping through a last wave like a dropped hula skirt
to return to this corral of dullards and oafs; layabouts.
Having survived an indifferent sea
that's perpetually washing its hands of remotest concern
(responsibility) for either herself or pup.

      — *Hey Mum!*, whelp barks:
      Here look! Feed me!
Dive-tackling her, as she sidles her way bone-wearily in:

still catching her wind, and a little stunned by this fury and fuss.
Arrived like the sea's tuck-shop.
Mrs fish-breath and lush dairy-dugs,
the sea's rompy-poley milk truck.

3 Male Australian fur seals basking

Great outsized slugs: limbless creatures
posed proud, with heads raised and necks arched,
besotted with the pure, pampered style of themselves.
Like so many Beau Brummells saluting the sun,
as they loll, indisposed, on backs or sides.
Upon shingle or sand,
or thrown themselves out at full length
to couch-surf the big, flat rocks.

Their lids half-closed over glazed eyes:
seeming comatose almost —
or like they've taken a Mafia-style hit,
one neat, clean bullet in the back of the head.
Laid there still as the sea's road-kill.

Which in fact would explain the smell:
for in the clear, acetylene-blue burning day
this place reeks like the rankest pissoir.
How can creatures that spend so much time in the water
stink a place up so much?

4 The garage

The dark rocks at Admiral's Arch sealery
are pooled with custardy oil-spills —

with the seals set up on blocks,
being tinkered at by the sun:

serviced and maintained,
making these running-repairs to themselves
to be slipped back onto the sea's road again.

5 Sea lion comes running

Flub-hobbling so eagerly
from sea up onto land,
the sea lion comes slap-clapping its way at us,
on its broken knees and hands.
A great-quivering, slobbering ball,
like the pet pooch of the Michelin-Man —
and consumed, it seems, with imperative news of some sort,
like some fish-breathed Paul Revere.

You wonder at the inordinate cost
that the creature brings on itself,
donning this mantle of clumsiness here —
slopping half-sidewards, to galumph ever-nearer,
hobbled, be-whiskered, half-blind.
With its better and sleeker, far more competent self
left sloughed off in the sea behind.

How close should we let the thing get to us?
(Has it violent intent? Should we be alarmed?)
With its skin tugged hard down over its bullet-head
like a stick-up man's pantyhose.
            Is it going to bash-and-rob us, or what?

6 *Envoi*

As we re-cross 'The Passage' back to the mainland,
three dolphins course at the car-ferry's bow,
heads half-turned, looking up at us with strained smiles —
like they're tugging the boat
with the sea's bit gripped in their mouths ...

As Port Jervois's wind-turbines reel us in,
and the mainland waits with crossed arms at the wharf ...
And we nose our way down off the ramp,
to find the road pointing us north
at sedate, straight-laced Adelaide now.

With things suddenly swung back around:
the fabulous, glittering island shrunk in the distance
like a brief, impetuous fling.
A week-long liaison of no lasting consequence,
put behind us now
as we're married to the mainland again.

Multicultural: the bore baths

Lightning Ridge, 1998

The Great Artesian Basin
has so many holes sunk in it these days
that it leaks like a sieve;
its lifting pressure in mortal decline.
Still, these bore baths survive, like an open-cut Jacuzzi
out here on the settlement's dark, scrappy edge.
Unfenced, and open 24/7 — free access for all.
A communal soak for locals and tourists alike,
with all the casual ambience of the lounge bar back in town.

And when you lift your eyes
to the big-black, alien, western-plains skies
cartwheeling overhead:
it's like a cave-in which might asphyxiate you,
stuffing your ears-mouth-and-nostrils with stars ...

As half of Mittel Europe seems gathered here tonight
                (Balts, Hungarians, Poles,
                                Czechs, Greeks, Yugoslavs).
Miners raised themselves from their day's dusty work,
some in company with their wives —
ranged pink and steaming through open pores
as they loll, elbows up, hugging the round bath's side.
Looking in at each other, faces creased with peace.

And if one of these men lifted their hooded eyes
to the tsunami of star-whirl overhead,
they might conceivably think that the Milky Way
was the biggest strike they could ever find.
And the only one in their whole lifetime

they'd ever really need to make.
      (Coming moreover, like these baths, for free.)

Though of course there's actually bugger-all chance
of their electing to see things that way —
as they submerse theirself slowly, hippo-wise:
the bore water lapping warmly up over the lobes of their ears,
then higher to cover their head.

Mayday on the Tableland (Ancient Mariner)

New England, NSW, 1995

A kilometre above the sea,
     three hours inland,
he drifts the paddock's dun-coloured feast
of granite, basalt and trap.
In this sixth official year of drought.
Alone, in his stump-tailed Ferguson.

His rock harvest sits piled at the paddock's edge.
The fenceline's dumb, shipped oars
signalling *Mayday* ...
As he comes up to the turn,
and stops.

Wipes his cracked, dry lips backhand
and looks to where the trees die-back
into the distant range.

Then guns the engine, nudges into gear,
continues his slow, harrowing work.

     Caught in the entrails of the beast.
     El Nino's arrow put clean through the albatross.

     Sole guest at this mean feast,
     upon the high, dry tableland.

Paradise now

'This parrot is no more! ... 'E's shuffled off 'is mortal coil [and]
joined the bleedin' choir invisible!' — *Monty Python*

Land clearance, grazing and changed patterns of burning
depleted my native grasslands.
And this, in hand with feral predations,
the aviarists' avid egg-collecting
and my own perhaps perverse inclination
for building my nests in termite mounds
(to be pillaged and crushed for your tennis courts' surfacings)
proved a killer combination in the end ...

I have flown — am aetherised now,
with no space for regret or romantic reconstruction.
Profess to lament my absence if you will,
we both know that as ever you'll continue to blunder your way
across the face of this earth. (On your wing-&-a-prayer.)
As replacement birds serve as substitutes
for my beauty, colour, allure.
For so long as they survive too.

Don't pretend you'll miss my call,
which you hardly had time to record after all.
('A plaintive *tit-sweet* with sharp *queek* when alarmed,'
as evoked in the books ...
Looking back on it now, I'd have done well to have put out
more alarmed 'sharp queeks' at the time.)

In the way of such things (*vide* the Thylacine, *vide* Elvis)
occasional claims will be made for my sighting.
       At the Burnett River in Queensland —
       south over the border at Inverell.
       At a petrol station — in a cinema foyer —

at a drive-through fast-food chain ...
But these can be safely ignored:
the Paradise Parrot has left the building;
is 'dead, buried and cremated' — incontestably gone
to join song with the chorus of fellow-fletched species
privileged for extinction from this earth.
> (Like the Dodo, the Great Auk,
> the Moa, and the Passenger Pigeon.
> The Mascarene Coot, the Chatham Penguin...
> And the Laughing Owl —
> which is not laughing now, at all.)

And multiple more, all left their awkward page in the Bird-Book
to glare back at you like a Wall of Shame.
Or presently circling in holding pattern,
on cue for extinction too. [†]

It's a simple matter of brutal, cold logic:
birds of a feather flock together
for so long as sustainable conditions prevail.
Then their business ceases to prosper,
the species' numbers decline and the enterprise fails.

So: ...Elvis has left the building, okay?
With a splendid psittacine perched on one jump-suited shoulder:
> a bird with aqua-coloured breast
> embellished with scarlet flashes —
> red patches set high on its chocolate wings,
> brilliant turquoise rump
> and long, gracile, bronze-green tail ...
And there is no Paradise now.

May the experience prove salutary to you.
Make hay for the glittering moment the weather holds, Sunshine ...

As you and your fellow non-fledged kind
continue to transact your way through this treacherous world.

---

† Like the Painted Snipe, and the Hooded Plover —
the Orange-Bellied Parrot, the Night Parrot,
the Superb, the Swift and Gold-Shouldered Parrots —
to name a sample few. (Sometimes, I swear,
you could be excused for thinking extinction's
an exclusive psittacine prerogative;
a peculiar parrot affair.)

Rude meditations (shorts)

Antarctic exit

The Australian Antarctic Division
is shipping all the huskies home,
since they're classified as 'Introduced'.
But then so are the humans too.

Simulacra

Weird, how the representation of a thing —
a painting say, a photograph, or reproduction in a book —
often seems more riveting
than the actual Thing itself.

Edith Piaf retires from breadmaking

'— Non, Je ne me baguette rien.'

Linguistics residential, Byron Bay

[*Sing:*] 'We're all going on a …
         summer Halliday…'

Accession

When the Allies imposed harsh treaty terms
on the Germans at Versailles,
Hitler was in-Führiated.

Forest Spirit haiku

Pine-tree chainsawn to its stump,
cones scattered on the ground all round:
        knackered Forest Spirit.

La guillotine: a defence

If they'd intended to be mean
when they designed the guillotine,
they'd have made you lie facing up.

Reciprocal

water fowl:
        flying fishes.

Life reflections

1
Your life is recorded in your children
like the rings in a tree.

2
Life is good.
And in any case is all you'll get.

3
'Shape up or ship out!', Life said.
But alas he slipped up
and got shat out by Life instead.

Vale (from the Crematorium's Annual Report)

This year, in a company milestone,
the firm's founding-director went up in smoke.

Sunfish variations

1
Sailing his yacht by pale moonlight
he crashed head-on into a sunfish.

2
Given the number of incidents you hear
of a yacht damaging its steering gear
on a sunfish:
how many sunfish could actually be floating out there
for the bloody yachts to collect?

Renal

'Your urine should have the colour of champagne,'
the Indian intern archly states
giving a pucker of his mouth —
as if, up till now,
he's been drinking Dom Pérignon Vintage all his life.

Interview with an astronaut

In the entire, hour-long interview
the man never makes a single joke
nor passes the least ironic comment.
Which is precisely why
he's an astronaut,
of course.

On the ward (a real-life event)

When the old Italian hacks sputum into a tissue
to ponderously consider it,
then hails a passing nurse to inquire:
'Does this look *normal*? To *you*?!'

she grimaces, 'Ooh!-*Arrggh*!', and says:
'Put it away please Marko won't you,
I haven't had my dinner yet!'

Grand touring

Kingsford Smith airport, May 2015

When our ecologist daughter flies in
from her Central America cycling tour,
we expect her to come through Customs
with an armadillo on a lead, at least.
A howler monkey perched on one shoulder?
A sloth clinging at her knees?

But what she brings back are her tired smiles,
two dirty, full-packed bicycle paniers,
and a bottle of Patrón Tequila duty-free.

A 'Suitable Boy': monastic succession in an Age of Terror

'Beijing and the exiled Dalai Lama are at odds in nominating the boy successor to the recently deceased 10ᵗʰ Panchen Lama, second highest Tibetan religious authority.' —newspaper article

Act I

i

Guided by ancient, occult rituals, the posse of senior monks searches for the Panchen's reincarnation in the form of a six-year-old boy. Scrying the surface of the great oracle lake *Lhamo Latso* through binoculars for portents and clues, before breaking to take their *tsampa* and buttered tea. One monk grabs a smoke and unwinds with the *Times* cryptic crossword, while the driver checks messages on their sat-phone — before all climb back into the LandCruiser to continue the pursuit.

ii

Somewhere Mao has warned: *'A single spark might start a prairie fire.'*

Sub-text: Keep Tibet on tight rein. Watch that treacherous snake, Taiwan. And muzzle the Muslim Xinjiang provinces: ... Insurrectionists, separatists and degenerate revisionists of every stripe and kind lurk everywhere. Be prepared to break heads.

iii

From exile, the Dalai Lama announces his own boy-choice to the world: whom Beijing immediately repudiates as a despicably

*Un*suitable Boy (son of notorious speculators, scramblers after fame and profit) — to nominate their own. Then fast-track him through the traditional four-year training program, climaxed with a ceremony on state TV in which Beijing's Suitable-Boy nominee is bewilderedly led to his throne. He exchanges white silk scarves with the President, who whispers the essential State koans in his ear: upholding of the 'Patriotic Spirit', and 'Sacred Unity of the Motherland'. ('One China above all, Suitable-Boy — understand?')

Off-screen meanwhile, for the Dalai Lama's Boy, things have turned increasingly grim. Eventually he and his whole family, along with the search-party's leading abbot, have all been disappeared.

Act II

A backwoods cabin, high on the Karakoram Range

A young, mohawked monk tosses his spent Marlboro to the ground to crush under the heel of his yak-skin hunting boot. Thumbs a handful of saffron-painted cartridges into a bandolier — slips a sawn-off shotgun in behind the drivers seat of his SUV, and with its speakers blasting 'Bat Out of Hell' full-bore, guns off up the Siddhartha Highway, cutting north-east ...

As he crosses above *Lhamo Latso* at dusk, the lake boils with fish floating belly-up; then slowly turns incarnadine. And he's lost in a slurry of gravel over the furthest ridge, dust billowing in his wake; like incense pumped from ten-thousand angry censers, or a warehouse of prayer-flags put to the flame. An *Om mani padme hum* amulet kicks at his rear-view mirror. And a bumper-sticker winks:

> *Sometimes one god*
> *must pluck out the eye*

of the other god
so both can breathe.

As, up on the Roof-of-the-World, one monk's combat-boot waits for the sound of the second combat-boot to drop, and detonate the avalanche.

The Nazis, the beaches

1 Traudl Junge at Noosa: the sea, the sun, the dictationist

Traudl Junge, Hitler's personal dictationist, visited her sister in Australia in the
1970s — holidaying with her on the Queensland coast and reportedly applying
for residency (newspaper report)

Three decades on, she sits smoking a menthol cigarette
on a Noosa beach. Hair neatly pinned in a bun.
At 50, she prides herself on still being able to wear
a two-piece swimsuit.
And as her sister says, she always had the legs.

Downhearted of late, she's enjoying this break
from tired-grey Europe — has made some friends,
is taking a pottery class, and is generally feeling quite good in herself.
Content. Yes, Australia fits her well —
like this new, floral-patterned swimsuit.
It's hard to be glum when the sun shines so big,
benign and strong: the waves lift-and-fall in little blue, languid,
sun-dazzled salutes; and the blond sand squeaks cleanly underfoot.
So it seems there's hope yet to re-find — redefine — yourself
in a southern clime. With all that dark-pressing history left spilt
behind,
like so much water flown under the Glienicke Bridge...

Yes, if the Past is another country, as said,
she'd be happy to live in this one now thanks.
Given the ASIO clearance and go-ahead ...

As her shoulders start to burn, and she takes a last drag
on her cigarette, pushes it face-down in the sand.

Snaps her bathing cap on — stands, and saunters light-hipped
toward her sister and niece who wave from the surf.

One life might bear all manner of strange fruit.
As it does for this ex-Hitler girl:
the dictator's dictationist, at 22.
And now showing a leg here at Noosa, thirty years on.
Still looking good in a two-piece swimsuit.

2 A *berghof* at Byron

Barring considerations of 'Destiny'
          (accidents of history, circumstance and birth)
he'd have quite liked it here, I think …

Imagine if you will: a *berghof* at Byron.
Some simple, bungalow-style getaway
with unspoilt coast views;
where he could tug off his jackboots
to flex his pale feet in the sand at the edge of the sea.

Strictly speaking the idea's quite fanciful, I grant:
a little *bescheuert* and *ziemlich absurd*.
Pretty well out of left field.
Still, let's just entertain ourselves if we can:
for who knows how all this bracing salt-air and ozone
away from the grey malaise of Berlin
and the chill, damp Alpine mountains and *wald*
might have cured him of his *melancholie* and *weltschmerz*.
Purged his heavy, sorry heart-and-head.
And where things might all have ended then?

Of course it's true, as they say:
'If "ifs" and "buts" were candy and nuts

we'd all have a fine, merry Christmas.' But *still*:
we live and learn, yes? And standing here now,
it's enticing to imagine it …
As the dusk bleeds into the spindrift
which enfolds the Cape Byron lighthouse
to fuse land and sea into one piercing, grand,
blue-and-rose-coloured *anschluss* …
And a sea eagle wheels its way juddering in
without ruffling a single breast feather,
to feel its way along the cliff edge …

Yes, it's something you can almost taste I swear:

      The Fuhrer, stood here barefooted.
      Trouser legs rolled to his plump, white calves,
      field tunic unfurled …
      For once at peace, and in full command of himself.
      As he clutches a small, dripping bucket of pipis
      dug from Byron's aching, blond sand.

North Coast raps

Pacific Highway double-haiku

Driving the highway north,
you wonder by their number
whether it's cattle or *egrets*
that farmer is producing
in his autumn field —

as the tanned road-worker
with the red 'SLOW' sign
glances in through the windscreen at you:
looking peeved —
as if you have interrupted his surf.

'Seabank', sunrise. (Rapprochement)

Yamba

'Seabank' tilts its big, wooden deck at the sea:
the cliff-face upon which the house is built
being so steeply raked that the surf seems to break
on the pilings underneath ...

As three surfers drift abreast, facing east,
to the sun's great-blazing ball.
Each hipless, astride his board.
Sat in his circle seat to dawn,
as the sea's long-silky indolence
        billows, sidles,
                slides, slips-tips —
                        and then falls away under him.

Not enough to excite him to his feet,
to try dancing his board upon it, at all.
But just sit and contentedly watch,
arms folded across his chest.
Cupped in the Tasman's crimson-gleaming hands.
In this grand rapprochement:

> surfers asking nothing of the sea;
> the sea asking nothing of them.

'Pacific' (so-called)

'Pacific' Ocean, as you are called,
can't you be just a little more quiet — considerate —
as we sleep by the open window, please.
Almost deafened by your sound
as you run the surf in,
ram-raiding the shore below.

So we wonder what manner and scale of machinery
could induce or sustain you
across all the earth's beaches. Great, and small.

Why such ceaseless, pitiless battering-and-pounding
has not ground down all the world.

At Crescent Head Surfing Reserve

1 Laird of the waves (Silverback)

Pilgrimage has been made to this spot since the 1950s,
as first stop heading north out of Sydney
in search of the perfect wave.
And at this brisk, bracing 6 am,
a few veterans in skanky, grey ponytails,
and looking to have jemmied their bodyshape
into reluctant wetsuits,
sit bobbing off the point still.
Maybe riding their same longboards from 1968.

Others elect to sit warm in tracksuits
in the front seats of their vans,
boards safely strapped to the roof,
to contemplate working themselves up to it.
Beach branded deep into brown, wrinkled foreheads,
faces collapsed in dreamy smiles
as they gaze at the point.

Off which the greybeard in the sky-blue wetsuit
(a present for his 70th last year) —
and a gun surfer here decades-back,
when all the fresh-faced 40-year-olds huddled around him now
were still wet behind their ears —
has obviously got respect ...
As he dispenses the occasional, sage nod,
sat privileged there at the phalanx's head,
for first shot at the next-coming wave.

Come evening, you imagine him holding court
in the yuppified hotel-bistro over the road,

retailing the legend of the great Californian pioneers
who brought the first Malibu balsa-boards to Australia
at the time of the Melbourne Olympics in 1956.
Back in surfing's primordial years.
Then, finished his midi of low-strength beer,
raising himself to shuffle home
to his daughter's house on the hill.
To kiss his grandchildren's foreheads
and help slip them off to bed.

2 The caravan park

From the beach you can float on your back in the creek,
and be carried a quarter-kilometre upriver by the tide —
up under the old, white wooden footbridge
alongside the caravan park …
And then, on the ebb, be carried equally nimbly back.

And by 9.30 pm, a fish-hook could be heard to drop in the place,
with all the seniors tucked in bed
to be up for their dawn fish or surf.
The entire scene as gently astonishing
as the sight of the camping family's pet rabbit
with its silver-studded, crimson collar
nonchalantly nibbling the grass alongside their tent.
            (Hip-hop —
                    hop-hip. *Whisker-tremble. Sniff* …
                                            Hop-hip …)

Yes, the most marvellous gentleness rolls through this place
on perpetual loop — like the sea when the swell has dropped,
and the wavelets come tripping: tipple-topple
their tinker-tanker way in …
rippling the estuary like the breeze in an Aeolian harp's strings.

And again — if you want — you can wade out into the creek.
Lie flat on your back and let your body go limp
for the incoming tide to benignly bear you along
its full length in moonlight.
Up under the perfect, white crescent-arc
of the wooden footbridge.

3 Grey nomads *manqués*

These old codgers in their vans
would make wonderfully adept Grey Nomads:
if, back in the first place that is, at least,
on arrival here 40 years ago,
they'd ever actually managed to leave.

West Australian pieces

Indemnity: the flensers

On a 1970s photograph in the Albany Whaling Museum

These fit-looking, young men
with strong, bared upper-arms,
in blue singlets and stubbie shorts,
look all set for a game of AFL —

but each wears gumboots
with spiked cleats at the heel;
and is carrying the strange-looking hockey stick
of his flensing tool.

The caption tells that because of the site's whirring blades,
pulleys and hooks, and tangle of chains
on the blood-slippery floor,
no company would insure this work —

just as the whales, ditto —
plying their dangerous trade in the blue sea every day
in the course of their own livelihood —
went their way un-indemnified too.

Serendipity blues (Another real-life story)

Alexandra Bridge camp, Blackwood River

Scarlet-breasted robin
in the riverside peppermint tree
under which I sit cooling my feet —

please explain why: in all of this state's
2.6 million square-kilometre spread,
you poop precisely on *me*.

Mon semblable, mon frère (not): Wave Rock

Two hundred kilometres in from the sea,
this rock would have not the remotest concept
of its constituting a 'wave' —

just as no wave
would be remotely induced to recognise (or accept)
this concave-shaped, granite rock in the desert
as confrère.

Embraer E-190 Blues: random thoughts flying home east

If this plane crashed head-on,
then — after the cockpit crew —
first-class would get taken out first at least,
I commiserate myself.
Waiting forever back in Economy
for the meal trolley to squeeze its way through.

And of all the people of this earth,
this bloke working his laptop's spreadsheets
in number 20E
would be the one I'd die alongside of.
        (Might he be a fit-and-proper person for the task?
        Should I ask for a change of seat?)

In any case — working the odds —
four hours later we've landed back east.

      'Flight crew, disarm cabin doors,'
      the intercom squawks
      (the crew presumably being trained
      in the appropriate close-quarter combat techniques).

      While we passengers get cautioned to exercise care
      when opening our overhead lockers,
      for any treacherous items shifted in flight.

Sweet Christ, I think to myself,
bowing my head out the aircraft's door:
it's small miracle we get our great gawping feet
planted safely back down on the ground at all.

The Earlwood jap pumpkin (The nourishing)

The jap pumpkin's markings are subtle and handsome
as our prize tabby cat's. The hard, grey-green skin,
mottled brown, with lime-splotch,
has a dulled-chromium sheen;
with a fine, jagged, yellow-gold thread like a racing stripe
running down one side of it.

Swelled with the Sydney sun, it sits squat and round-hipped
on our kitchen bench. The size of a potentate's paunch.
Seeming well-satisfied with itself.
(Smug you might say, almost.)
And when you slip the carving knife's tip
into the gnarly, umbilical centre of it
to draw the big handle,
                    guillotine-wise,
                        slowly down:
it suddenly gives with the resounding, ear-pleasing crack
of good, seasoned firewood.
To tell that it's ripe for the pot.

Its gold-yellow flesh produces a delicious, honey-sweet, nut-
flavoured soup.

> *Shear off the rind, cut the flesh into wedges,*
> *then dice into cubes … Boil with sliced apple then blend,*
> *and reheat with thin-sliced, fried bacon strips.*
> *Serve up with crusty, lavishly buttered bread.*

Yes, my word: we should all feel as bounteous, blessed
and solidly earthed as this pumpkin produced
from a friend's inner-west Sydney backyard,
after a season of plentiful sun and rain.

Then cut from its stalk and let sit to mature a while
on a laundry window-ledge.
Before having its pieces ceremoniously slung
into a royal blue cast-iron cooking pot
to create such a nourishing soup as this.

Ornithology on the Cook River at Earlwood

The Cook River sidles its methaney-way on
through industrial-urban mangrove;
like Sherwood Forest in a spittoon.
As we're walking the cycle path
between afternoon soccer fields.
And the talk is Poetry:
when I ask whether Homer Street
could really be named for the poet,
you say you believe it's true.
(As a Jumbo screams in low,
streaming grey kerosene upon the bard's head ... Surreal!)

Meanwhile, the back-gardens of the inner-west's million-dollar
houses reach their way down to us.
In one, a curly-haired man leans dreamily on a rake,
poised in reflection as he cleans the leaves from his pool.
Then, just beyond that, we pass a bird
perched on a post on the opposite bank.
Its colour and shape cleaved by sunburst.
We each hazard a guess what it is:
your call is cormorant; mine is heron.
But each being without our spectacles,
both judgements are suspect in any case,
so we let the matter stew.
As the Cook sidles its green-brown, methaney-way on.
And we continue ours ...

At the footbridge, you complain that when cycling here
the dog-walkers step right out in front of you
when you sound your bell from behind.
(It so pisses you off.)
And, riding here once after heavy rain,

you hit a big puddle, dropped your bike
and waterplaned three-metres sidewards.
Losing your glasses. (The same you're not wearing now.)

We cross Homer Street (whether the poet or not)
to take lattés at the Adora Café.
Along with a single, bespoke, jewel-like chocolate
we each nominate from a glass showcase.
(My word, do I eat this pretty, little thing,
or dangle it at the side of my nape?) ...

Then, walking back, we pass the contentious bird-place again.
(Cormorant? Heron? ... Shag? Bittern? ... Crane?).
But both being civilised men — with wives, daughters
and substantially mortgaged real estate —
who harmlessly prattle poetry while sauntering a cycle path
in the amiable, inner-west afternoon —
we don't reignite the debate.
The bird's flown now, anyway.
And life's too short to split feathers or hairs
over species of waterbird;
whether here on the Cook River at Earlwood
or any other place.
(When a heron, in essence, might just be considered
a cashed-up cormorant in any case.)

And so we turn from the path,
leaving the Cook to kick its way on.
As another Jumbo screams its way in,
low over Homer Street,
to sting the bard's eyes in a kerosene mist.

The ice-calf (Takes 1 & 2)

Take 1: Omniscient point-of-view (the berg, the ship, the sea)

Glaciologists calculate the berg would have taken three years to ride the ice chute down its Greenland slipway — then calve, and topple into the bay: Launching itself. The same amount of time it took Harland & Wolff's Belfast yard to construct the White Star Line's big steel ship.

The prevailing current would have initially courted the berg north-east, before pirouetting south: to duly find itself arrived at the crossroads just in time for the big, four-stacked ship to come tripping past. Humming along in the calm, moonless night, in the high-Edwardian rave of itself. Wrapped in its warm fug of cigar smoke. With its upper-deck orchestra, champagne and game-tables set over the simpler, cribbed life of the decks below. And so lit-up that it hardly saw the 12-storey-tall berg sidle idly into view — then loom like the ship's own great, white hand, held out before its own bright-brazen face.

Thus the two forces met. Ice-mass versus steel. Glacier-born versus man-made. Each mass waylaid for a quarter-minute or so as the other's energy registered, was absorbed and transferred. The ship juddering and screeling along its full length. The nudged berg sending crockery-sized ice-shards skittering and clattering onto the ship's decks — while its big, hidden spur dug deep, to rip and buckle the underbelly of steel-plate below ... Then, abruptly, the masses disengaged. Stabilised, to each resume its separate, sovereign course: ... The ship mortally wounded (as yet unknown to itself). The ice hurt too, to a conceptual degree (shed some miniscule mass; mildly stained with red anti-fouling paint). Then the current reasserted its grip, dragging the berg on its tarrying way ...

And three hours later, when the full calamity of the event was rung
— And the big ship faltered, and angled, then finally, stupendously,
upended and slid down by its head — and the handful of lifeboats
meagrely bloomed, bled and spidered whitely out across the chill,
empty-echoing pond, to limp away — the berg, with its dark part in
the fable played, continued its leisurely cruise. Mooching south to the
sun's waiting breaking-yard. Released back into its own recognisance;
licensed to be pure, brute ice again ... And over the subsequent
fortnight or so, geophysicists say — by which time likewise the
bodysearch to the north was long done — it would have wasted itself
from the dimensions of a brownstone apartment-block, to those of a
bungalow; then a pool-table, then a ship's wheel — and finally to a
bone-china dinner-plate. Too small to ever trace. Implicate or blame...
And then — like the ship — the berg was stolen cleanly from view.
Disposed of by the sea, like the murder weapon in the perfect crime.

Take 2: Subjective point-of-view. (The subpoenaed berg defends itself before the Inquiry)

Really, what was I to do — as the big, lame-lit thing came lumbering
at me; gormlessly, head-on. And I clung, locked into the current, in
flagrant full-view. There, in the traditional playing fields and accepted
latitudes. Migrating southward: in the place where, for all time, the
prevailing currents have borne bergs to ...

It was a calm, clear night. We were arrayed in a thin, scattered pack
any competent ship could navigate itself through. With so much open
sea as buffering zone all round ... Yet perversely the thing chose to
directly cross my path — deliberately seek me out, almost.

I recall, on approach, the sense perhaps of some small, late animal
panic aboard. A clumsy, late-feinted manoeuvre: the bow commencing

to turn, the propellers belatedly put on high-boil ... And then, when the contact came, I absorbed it in the only manner I could and was capable of: mass-to-mass; bulk-ice to bulk-steel ... Ballasted and configured as I was. With no manoeuvre to pull to retreat from the field; disengage, withdraw or detach myself.

And in truth, only the most minor scuffle ensued: a mere glance, a nudge or bump ... I recall the brief sight of a host of small, pale, passing faces, lime-lit and stood gawping at the rail. A few seemed amused, gathering pieces of ice to let fly at each other, dancing little jigs in some kind of game ... As already the big-thrumping, four-stacked thing was bustling on, dragging its great avalanche-tail behind, the width of five tennis courts. Tripping heartily westward. And, last I saw, still looking tall, haughty and full of itself. Utterly composed. Playing 'to-the-manner-born'. Ablaze in its great glassy hornet's nest of illumination: lit up like half of Pall Mall. With its four big black stacks, each pumping fat-greasy plumes of smoke like a card-party of cigar-toking plutocrats ... Then its great, snowy wake was sutured over in a neat, glassy scar, and then finally smoothed away. The clear, calm night folding over the thing: diminishing it to a pinprick of light, before blacking it wholly from view ... And so I was left alone again, with all I had ever asked for: the quiet night, with the masterful current reasserted itself, and the chill, star-pocked sky. To pursue my course unobstructed; as assigned. Drifting my southward way.

And that's all I can say, for however much it's of use to you. Though I would state that I resent the implication that I was complicit in this loss of life in some way. The bandied sense of vilification — of being somehow to blame. For in truth I had no presentiment at all of the tragic events to ensue. And would simply declare before this Inquiry, that I am as entirely confounded by the whole extraordinary business as you.

The shark, the arm

A Noh-style monologue: Woman speaker in 1930s era clothing and whiteface

We met at the Coogee Palace Aquarium Baths. I used to catch the
number 37 tram back from work in the city, see. Get off at the beach
for a breath of fresh air, chase the collywobbles out before walking up
the hill home. Having a look at Wylie's Baths — that's a tidal pool.
They were the swimming champions: Mina Wylie, she got the silver at
the Stockholm Olympics. Freestyle. In 1912, I think. But it's 1935 that I
want to talk about now. And I was only seventeen back then, just a little
Miss. But sassy in my way. And I remember the day I met Merv as clear
as a bell.

There was a chalk-board, see, set up on the promenade. Saying to pay
sixpence to go in for a look at some shark they'd caught in the nets. So I
paid up and in I went. And there it was: a genuine, professional-looking
brute; a nasty piece of work. Blue whaler I think. Or maybe a tiger?
Looking happy as a sand-boy in there, with this big fin poking up,
cruising round the tank as smooth as silk. Three and a half metres long
it said. (That was over 10 foot back then, before the metrics they got
now.) And so I'm stood there getting my full sixpence-worth, watching
this brute knock its way round its tank. Feeling pretty happy to be
stood up in the dry myself, instead of down in the water flopping about
with him. And then finally, just as I'm turning to nudge my way out
on home, the wretch comes on a bit 'agitated', you'd say. Weaving and
banging into the sides of the pool, like one of them carnival dodgem-
cars. Then hoves itself into a corner right under where yours truly is
stood, to hunker down for a bit of a sulk. With the sick look of a bunny
with myxo, caught up against a fence. And then, suddenly, it gets the
full heebie-jeebies, like it's wired up to the mains. And I can see that
it's vomiting something up. In a sort of burley, like you'd sling from a
bucket out the back of a boat to catch the big fish, you know. Blood and
gore, shrimp bits, white-tail and such — in among which is something

that looks like someone's chewed-up long socks. And then, my stars! My eyes are falling out of my head! Cause I'm suddenly seeing a *human arm*! Floating there naked as day. Right in the middle of it!

A whole *human arm*, would you credit that?! Whether right or left I couldn't say, and it's hardly the point in any case. But it was taken off neat as a pin, I can tell you that. High up at the shoulder, just as clean as if our corner butcher had done it. And it had a blue *tattoo*. Imagine that! Well, I didn't know whether to laugh or cry — to smirk, or scream, or *puke* for that matter. Could have done all five by rights I should think, to be subjected to *that* sort of outrageous thing! (Afterwards Merv said he'd felt pretty ambiguous too. Shocked, just like me. So you could see there was something between us then, or we had something in common at least) ... But anyway: there we both were, watching this blue whaler (or maybe a tiger?) swimming about in the tank — and then suddenly, before you say 'Goose!', without a simple by-your-leave, the brute's heaved up a human arm. Completely unasked, and unashamed. Well, it *was* a bit rich I mean! And with just me and this nice-looking, neat-dressed young man stood there to witness it. (They all wore suits and hats back then, the men. Just for the everyday. Not like the way they dress now.) And *anyway*, this nice-looking fellow as I describe, with this new blue trilby on — Merv of course, as he turns out to be — walked over to stand close up by me at the rail. For a closer look. At the shark. Or me: to maybe check that I was all right, gentleman as he is. (Or he was back then) ...

But you know *another* interesting thing? That arm had a *watch*, still strapped on at the wrist. (So in fact the *left* arm, I guess I can now suppose it to be. Hadn't thought it through at the time.) But whether working or not, I couldn't say. Whether it kept proper time; which it could be excused for not doing in any case, given that drastic situation eh ... But Good Heavens, I'll never forget the sight of that arm, not as long as I live. Some things are made to stick in your mind. Or your brain. Like a chicken bone gets caught in your throat.

And a *floating arm*, with a *blue tattoo*, and a *wrist watch* still strapped onto it, whether keeping proper time or not — well, that's one of those 'memorable' sort of things my word!

So anyway: *that's* how me and Merv met, you see. Since you ask. At the Coogee Palace Aquarium Baths. In 1934 (or '35 was it?). And so, though the event, with one thing and another, was a fair bit of a shock at the time, things turned out good in the long run, didn't they? ...

Well — except for the poor bloke belonged to the arm, I suppose. And for whatever happened to the rest of him. And for the shark too I guess, in a way, if you're the kind to fret on such things. Cause they went and killed it after that, cut it open you see, to check. Well they *had* to didn't they. It only makes sense, just a natural response. And the police evidently got some fingerprints off it. The arm, that is. And his wife was able to identify him by the tattoo too, apparently. (And I guess maybe also by his watch?) And so *that* was fortunate as well. Though I'm not sure they ever actually managed to prosecute ... Anyway, it was quite a famous case in the day. Written up in all the newspapers. In the cinema newsreels and such.

But it *was* pretty outrageous really, the whole blessed thing. Life's amazing the way it works sometimes — or at least it makes you stop and think.

Acknowledgments

'The Human Stain (Rosalie Gascoigne)' won the David Campbell Prize 2011.

'Snake-man' won second prize, Rosemary Dobson Prize 2008.

'Induced-Birth Method' won second prize, Shoalhaven Poetry Competition 2010.

Some of these poems (often in different versions) have appeared in the following newspapers and journals: *Blue Dog, Hobo, Australian Poetry Journal, The Canberra Times, Meanjin online,* and *Cordite* ('Ekphrastic' edition); as well as in the chapbook of selected poems *Greenhouse: the Penguins Revolt & Other Poems* (Picaro Poets/ Ginninderra Press). And in the following anthologies: *The Invisible Thread: One Hundred Years of Words* (Canberra centenary anthology, 2012; ed Irma Gold); *The House Is Not Quiet And The World Is Not Calm: Poetry From Canberra* (2014; ed Kit Kelen & Geoff Page); and *Falling and Flying: Poems on Ageing* (2015; ed Judith Beveridge & Dr Susan Ogle). Websites: ArtsACT website; and Randwick Council's 'La Perouse' website. The dramatic monologue 'The Shark, the Arm' was performed and recorded at the Sydney Fringe Festival 2016, under the Spineless Wonders 'Little Fiction Call Out' program.

My thanks to David Musgrave. And to Andy Kissane, and Kirsty Morrison.

This book is for my parents, Arthur ('Bill') Cliff (1920-2012) and Gladys Joan Cliff (née Willetts) (1925-2014). And for my brother, Mark Cliff (1949-1955).

Notes to poems

'The Editor's Wife (Reprise)' is a radical recasting of 'Cry Freedom (The editor's wife: a letter)', from my earlier collection *The Impatient World*. 'Ode to Leo Fender' was developed from the documentary film *Curves, Contours and Body Horns — History of the Fender Stratocaster* (Ray Minhinnett, 1994) and its associated webpage. Musicians mentioned, quoted quite literally in some part, are respectively Keith Richards, Eric Clapton and Jimi Hendrix. 'Relieving the Camp' was developed from descriptions of the relief of Dachau Concentration Camp on 29 April 1945 and subsequent days, as provided at http://scrapbookpages.com/DachauScrapbook. 'Accountants at War' is developed from an article by Amanda Hainsworth, in *Charter: Journal of the Chartered Accountants of Australia*, August 1995. 'A Suitable Boy' was developed from an original article in the *Weekend Australian*, 3-4 Feb 1996, at p 5. 'The Eucalpyt Pod' was developed from facts given in Hugh Kenner's *The Pound Era*, at pp 171-72.